INTERPLAY

LISA ACK

INTRODUCTION

social behavior communication is the process of exchanging meanings between people through a common set of symbols.

The functions, forms, and psychology of communication are discussed in this article. See animal behavior for a discussion of animal communication. See language for additional discussion of the fundamental components and strategies of human communication; speech; writing. See broadcasting for technological aspects like information systems and communication devices; dictionary; encyclopedia; processing of information; knowledge theory; library; printing; publishing, its background; media for communication; network of communications; system for communication.

Since ancient Greece, scholars have been interested in the topic of communication. However, prior to the modern era, the topic was frequently incorporated into other fields of study and assumed to be a natural process that was inherent in each. I.A. Richards, an English literary critic and author, gave one of the first, and still one of the best, definitions of communication as a distinct aspect of human endeavor in 1928:

Although Richards' definition is broad and vague, its application to nearly all forms of communication, including those between humans and animals (but not machines), separated the contents of messages from the processes by which they are transmitted in human affairs. Recently, concerns have been expressed regarding the sufficiency of any given definition of the term "communication" in its current usage. Jurgen

Ruesch, an American psychiatrist and scholar, identified 40 distinct disciplinary approaches to the topic, including architectural, anthropological, psychological, and political interpretations of the seemingly straightforward interaction that Richards described. There are at least fifty distinct modes of interpersonal communication that draw on dozens of distinct intellectual disciplines and analytical approaches when including informal communications like sexual attraction and play behavior. Therefore, communication can be analyzed in at least fifty different ways.

Advances in science and technology, which by their very nature have brought attention to the fact that humans are creatures that communicate, have sparked interest in communication. The telegraph and the telephone were among the first and most significant examples of technological inventions, followed by wireless radio and telephoto devices. Institutional and cultural innovations that enabled quick and effective communication between a small number of people and large populations were made possible by the rise of popular newspapers, periodicals, broadcasting, movies, and television; The new phenomenon of mass communication's rise and social power are both due to these media. Additionally, information theory processing of information; system for communication.)

Since roughly 1920, the development of communications technology and its apparent influence have piqued the interest of numerous experts, who have attempted to isolate communication as a specific aspect of their research. In their studies of behavior and the mind, psychologists have developed communication concepts that are beneficial to both their investigations and certain types of therapy. Myths, ways of life, mores, and traditions are passed down from one generation to the next or from one section of society to another through a variety of methods of communication that have been identified by social scientists. Economists and political scientists have both recognized that the social order's regularities are rooted in a variety of forms of communication. Mathematicians and engineers have attempted to quantify and measure components of communicated information as a result of new technology, particularly high-speed computers, and to develop methods for translating various types of messages into quantities or amounts that are compatible with their instruments and procedures. Artists, architects, craftspeople, writers, and others have asked a lot of different questions about the overall effects of different forms of communication. Working within the relevant issues of their respective fields, a lot of researchers have also looked for theories or laws of cause and effect that could explain how certain kinds of communication affect human dispositions and why they change.

Marshall McLuhan, a Canadian educator, drew on the interests in the field of communication in the 1960s to propose a theory that linked a number of contemporary psychological and sociological phenomena to the media used in contemporary culture. Numerous filmmakers, photographers, artists, and others adopted McLuhan's view that contemporary society had moved (or was moving) from a "print" culture to a "visual" one and were inspired by his often-repeated concept that "the medium is the message." McLuhan and his followers were most interested in the specific forms associated with the sophisticated technological instruments that young people are particularly enthusiastic about, like movies, television, and sound recordings.

In the latter part of the 20th century, the main areas of interest in communication shifted away from McLuhanism and began to center on the following topics: (1) the mass communication industries, the people who run them, and the effects they have on their audiences; (2) persuasive communication and the use of technology to influence dispositions; (3) the processes of interpersonal communication as mediators of information; (4) the dynamics of verbal and nonverbal (and possibly extrasensory) communication between individuals; (5) perception of various types of communications;

In a nutshell, a communication specialist may specialize in any one of a number of fields within a field of study that has not yet established a comprehensive list of topics or agreed-upon specific analysis methods.

Models of communication fragmentation and issues with an interdisciplinary perspective have sparked a wide range of debate regarding the processes and modes of communication. The task of the communication theorist is to provide the most precise answer to the question, "Who says what to whom with what effect?" (The majority of speculation on these issues acknowledges this in one way or another). Harold D. Lasswell, a political scientist from the United States, originally asked this question.) Evidently, scholars and writers from various fields may interpret this question's key elements in different ways.

Linear models Claude Shannon and Warren Weaver, two American mathematicians, came up with one of the most useful schematic models of a communications system that has been proposed as an answer to Lasswell's question in the late 1940s. Although it is neither the only model of the communication process that exists nor is it universally accepted, many students of communication from a variety of fields found their model appealing due to its clarity, surface generality, and simplicity. The model originally had five linearly arranged components: an information source, a transmitter, a channel of transmission, a receiver, and a destination. This path was supposed to take messages—at first, electronic messages—from the transmitter to the receiver, where they would be transformed into electrical energy and reconstructed into language that could be understood. As time went on, the five parts of the model were given new names to indicate parts for other kinds of communication that could be sent in different ways. To provide a wider range of application possibilities, the information source was broken down into its component parts—the message and the source. The revised model is made up of six parts: a source, an encoder, a message, a channel, a decoder, and a receiver. The components of some communication systems are as straightforward as, for instance, a person on a landline telephone, the telephone's mouthpiece, the words spoken, the electrical wires along which the words (now electrical impulses) travel, the earpiece of another telephone, and the listener's mind. The parts of other communication systems are harder to separate—for example, the art of conveying a fine artist's feelings through a painting to people who might respond to the message long after the artist has passed away.

From a common sense perspective, at least, the linear model appeared to provide a general explanation for the ways in which particular classes of communication occurred. However, it also sparked a multitude of psychological, aesthetic, and sociological questions regarding the precise nature of each component. It didn't say why some communications that are obvious in everyday life didn't fit its neat paradigm.

Redundancy, negative entropy, and entropy were added to the communication model. Another idea, which Shannon initially referred to as a "noise source," was later linked to the idea of entropy, which is a physics principle. The majority of communication is analogous to entropy, which refers to external influences that compromise the integrity of the communication and may even distort the message for the recipient. This is analogous to static in audio or video. Negative entropy can also occur when incomplete or blurry messages are still received intact, either because the receiver is able to fill in the gaps or because they are able to recognize the message's intent and content despite distortion or a lack of information.

The greatest antidote to entropy is redundancy, which is the repetition of elements within a message that prevents the failure of information communication but is rarely shown on diagrammatic models of this version of the communication process. For instance, the majority of spoken and written languages are roughly half redundant. Even if 50 percent of the words in this article were taken out at random, the essay would still be understandable, if a little odd. Similarly, a radio news commentator's broadcast can typically be understood if only half of their words are heard. Redundancy is necessary for effective communication because it helps to overcome the various forms of entropy that tend to turn intelligible messages into unintelligible ones (including psychological entropy on the part of the receiver). Redundancy appears to be involved in the majority of human activities.

As a result, messages can be significantly altered and mediated. Negative entropy and redundancy, on the other hand, help to clarify; The likelihood of a message being received and correctly understood varies depending on how each component of the communication process operates in different ways. However, the fundamental focus of the process—along with its model—is on messages sent from point to point rather than their outcomes or potential effects on sender and receiver. As a result, the process and model remain conceptually static.

Feedback The principle of feedback was added to the model to address this flaw, providing a more realistic representation of interpersonal human interaction than was previously known. The research conducted by Norbert Wiener, dubbed the "father" of the field of cybernetics, provided the basis for this concept. Some of Wiener's cybernetic models, which form the basis of current computer technology, were created to respond to their own actions; Specifically, they audited their own performance mathematically or electronically to avoid entropy errors, redundant work, and other straightforward dangers.

Holiday greeting cards, for instance, typically require little feedback from recipients. The ability of the message sender to weigh and calculate the apparent effect of his words on his listener is essential for the functioning of others, particularly conversations between people. Because each instance of feedback conditions or alters the subsequent messages, it is largely the aspect of feedback that provides this model with the characteristics of a process.

Other dynamic models of communication processes have been created to meet the needs of communication students whose interests diverge from those of quantitative theorists like Shannon, Weaver, and Wiener. Although the aforementioned model exhibits some generality and simplicity, it lacks some predictive, descriptive, and analytical capabilities. For instance, a psychologist by the name of Theodore M. Newcomb developed a more fluid system of dimensions to represent how an individual interacts with his environment. Because Newcomb's model and others like it are not as mathematically (quantitatively) precise as Shannon's, they make it possible to account for human behavior in a more flexible way and its variable relationships. They don't deny that linear models are important to Shannon and Weaver's main concerns, which are the quantity of information and how messages are delivered under controlled conditions. However, they do question whether or not linear models are useful for describing the cognitive, emotional, and artistic aspects of communication in sociocultural matrices.

Students who focus on persuasive and artistic communication often focus on narrative, pictorial, and dramatic modes of communication and theorize that the messages they contain, including messages of emotional quality and artistic content, are communicated in a variety of ways to and from a variety of people. The stability and function of the channel or medium are less mechanistically related to the process for them than they are for Shannonians, Weavers, and psychologists like Newcomb. In point of fact, McLuhan asserts that the channel dictates or significantly influences the message as it is sent and received.) The nature of messages, including their compatibility with sense and emotion, style, and intentions, is a topic of interest to many communication analysts, linguistic philosophers, and others. Despite the fact that considerations associated with these models, particularly those of entropy, redundancy, and feedback, have provided the majority of students of communication with significant and productive concepts, they find that linear and geometric models of process are of little interest to their concerns.

Applications of formal logic and mathematics
Despite the many different kinds of communication or information theory that exist today and are likely to be developed in the future, the constructions that Shannon and others described above are the most rationally and experimentally consistent approaches to communication theory that have been developed thus far. Instead of the looser syntaxes, grammars, and vocabulary of common languages with their symbolic, poetic, and inferential aspects of meaning, these approaches typically employ the structural rigors of logic.

In order to enable translation into distinct, unambiguous symbols that can be stored and utilized for statistical manipulations, both computer technology and the theory of cybernetics require rigorous yet simple languages.

For this purpose, formal logic's closed system proved to be ideal. As long as all parties communicating agree on the rational premises utilized by the particular system, it is simple to test in a consistent, scientific manner the premises and conclusions drawn from syllogisms in accordance with logical rules.

It was inevitable that this logical method of communication derived its discourse framework from the logic of the ancient Greeks. Meaningful interactions between people could be transferred to a mathematical closed system that is just as rational as the Aristotelian dialectic: an algebra for solving certain well-defined puzzles, an algebra for simple transactions, a calculus for simulating changes, rates, and flows, and a geometry for model construction and illustration. The limited classes of communications that result from certain structured, rational operations, such as those in economics, inductively oriented sociology, experimental psychology, and other behavioral and social sciences, as well as the majority of the natural sciences, have proven to be quite manageable with this progression.

The assumption that the transmitted message is well-organized, consistent, and characterized by relatively low and determinable degrees of entropy and redundancy is the foundation of the basic theorem of information theory. (If this were not the case, the mathematical structure might only produce probabilistic statements that are similar to random scatters and would be of little use to anyone.) It is possible to transmit symbols over a channel at an average rate that is nearly the capacity of units per second of the channel (symbolized by C) as a function of the units per second from an information source (H) under these conditions by devising appropriate coding procedures for the transmitter. However, no matter how expertly the symbols are coded, the rate will never exceed capacity divided by units per second (C/H). Even though this seems like a simple idea, precise mathematical models of information transactions, similar to electronic frequencies of energy transmissions, can be developed and used for complex analyses within the confines of formal logic after determining the channel's capacity and cleverly coding the information involved. Naturally, they must take into account all known variables and the highest possible levels of entropy and redundancy.

The above theorem's applicability is constrained by the channel's internal capabilities and the complexity of the information-handling coding procedures. Formal encoding procedures that are dependent on the capabilities of the instruments in which they are stored currently limit such procedures, despite the fact that they may theoretically offer broad prospects. The flexibility and complexity of the human brain, which continues to be the primary instrument for managing the subtleties of the majority of human communication, cannot be matched by such devices, despite their ability to quickly process vast amounts of information that is relatively straightforward.

Nonvocal communication is one type of communication. Signals, signs, and symbols are three related components of communication processes that are found in all known cultures. Because they do not primarily relate to the typical conception of words or language, they have attracted a lot of scholarly attention. Each seems to be a more and more complicated version of the first, and they probably developed long before or at the beginning of early human experiments with vocal language.

Signals A signal can be thought of as an interruption in a field where energy is constantly transferred. The dots and dashes that open and close a telegraph circuit's electromagnetic field are one example. The construction of a man-made field is not required for these interruptions; The same result may be achieved by natural interruptions, such as the tapping of a pencil in a quiet room or smoke rising from a mountaintop. Such signals' primary purpose is to change a single environmental factor in order to draw attention and convey meaning. A basic vocabulary of dots, dashes, or other basic audio and visual articulations can easily be developed into a code system that refers to interruptions in some meaningful way. The interruptions appear to have a very limited potential for meaning when taken on their own; They could be a sign that someone is in the room, a lack of patience, agreement, or disapproval with something about the environment, or, in the case of a scream for help, a serious situation that needs attention. They have a tremendous capacity for language communication and are coded to refer to spoken or written language.

Even though signs are usually less important to the development of words than signals are, most of them have more meaning on their own. An anthropologist by the name of Ashley Montagu has defined a sign as a "concrete denoter" with an inherent specific meaning, similar to the phrase "This is it; take action on it!" Pictures or drawings are the most common signs that people see every day, but a human posture like a clenched fist, an outstretched arm, or a hand posed in a "stop" position can also be a sign. The primary distinction between a sign and a signal is that a sign, like a policeman's badge, carries inherent meanings; A signal, like a scream for help, is nothing more than a tool for making up extrinsic meanings. The fact that many different kinds of animals respond to signals but only a few intelligent and trained animals, usually dogs and apes, are capable of responding to even simple signs shows their difference.

Signs are used by all known cultures to quickly and easily convey relatively straightforward messages. Signs' meanings may be affected by their shape, setting, color, or location. Traffic signs, uniforms, badges, and barber poles are all common signs in the United States. Any society's sign vocabulary is a rich vocabulary of colorful communications when taken collectively.

Symbols, in contrast to signs and signals, are intricately woven into an individual's ongoing perceptions of the world, making them more difficult to comprehend and define. As one of their functions, they appear to possess a capacity that, in fact, defines the world's very reality. Any tool that can be used to abstract something has been defined as a symbol. It leads in a profitable direction, despite not being a precise construction. Symbolism is based on the abstractions of values that people instill in other people and things they own and use. According to the British philosopher Alfred North Whitehead, this is a process in which, in Whitehead's view, symbols are analogues or metaphors (which can include written and spoken language as well as visual objects) that represent some quality of reality that is made more important or valuable by the process of symbolization itself.

Almost every society has developed a symbol system that gives strange things and strange behaviors the appearance of having irrational meanings and evoking strange, unjustified thoughts and feelings. Examining each symbol system reveals a distinct cultural logic, and each symbol serves the purpose of communicating information among members of the culture in a manner that is similar to but subtler than conventional language. Although a symbol can be as discrete as a wedding ring or a totem pole, symbols typically appear in groups and rely on one another to accumulate meaning and value. They are not an independent language; Instead, they are tools that people who have acculturated in similar ways use to spread ideas that are too difficult, dangerous, or awkward to say in common language. Because they lack the precision and regularities of natural language that are required for explicit definitions, it does not appear that discrete vocabularies of symbols can be compiled.

Icons Are typically regarded as rich clusters of related and unrelated symbols. They are actually groups of interactive symbols, like a funeral or Impressionist painting or the White House in Washington, D.C. Even though in examples like these, it's common to focus on specific icons and symbols for analysis, symbolic communication is so intertwined with all human endeavors that most people treat it as the most important form of social communication unconsciously. It is possible to comprehend the crucial roles that spoken and written words and numbers play in the fields of science, mathematics, literature, and art by realizing that they themselves function as symbolic metaphors. Additionally, these symbols enable an individual to define his or her identity.

Gestures Since ancient times, professional dancers and actors have known that body gestures can also create a language of communication that is more or less unique to each culture. Kinesics, an attempt to create a body language vocabulary, has been made by some academics in the United States. The findings of their research, which are both amusing and potentially useful, may one day lead to the creation of a real lexicon of American gestures that is comparable to one that was meticulously prepared by François Delsarte, a French pantomime and gymnastics instructor from the 19th century who described the ingenious and complex language of contemporary face and body positions used for theatrical purposes.

The theories that are involved in the study of proxemics, which were developed by an American anthropologist named Edward Hall, are of more general, cross-cultural significance. Proxemics is the study of how people from different cultures communicate by utilizing time, space, body positions, and other factors. The culturally determined interactions that make up Hall's "silent language" of nonverbal communications include the physical distance or closeness that people maintain between one another, the body heat that they emit, the odors that people perceive in social situations, the angles of vision they maintain while talking, the pace at which they behave, and the sense of time that is appropriate for communicating in various circumstances. Hall elaborated and codified a number of sophisticated general principles that demonstrate how certain kinds of nonverbal communication occur by comparing matters like these in the behavior of different social classes and relationships. The study of proxemics does succeed in drawing attention to significant aspects of communication dynamics that linguists and symbologists rarely consider, despite the fact that many of Hall's most impressive arguments are based almost entirely on empirical evidence. Words scholars have focused more on objective, formal vocabularies than on the subtler means of discourse that members of a culture unknowingly acquire.

Vocal communication There are more similarities than differences between vocal and nonvocal communication. Despite the fact that most people tend to think of signs, signals, symbols, and possibly icons as visual means of expression, there are times when they can be easily spoken. In some cases, vocalizations may also be involved in proxemics and kinesics as an accompaniment to or integral component of nonverbal phenomena. Whether they are grunts, words, or sentences, their purpose is to facilitate nonverbal communication.

The history of human speech is still a mystery, even though there is a lot of speculation about it. Man may be born with a speech instinct, which is plausible. The presence of infants' unlearned cries and gurgles, which function as crude vocal signs directed to others the baby cannot possibly be aware of, is a phenomenon that supports this belief. According to some anthropologists, the virtual building blocks of spoken language can be found within the vocabularies of proxemics and kinesics; They argue that primitive humans needed to communicate with others in order to pool their intellectual and physical resources, which necessitated the development of numerous inventive inventions, including speech. Other observers suggest that the vocalization of physical activity, mimicking the sounds of nature, and pure serendipity are all examples of similar origins for speech. At this time, there is no way for science to support any of these theories.

Experts disagree not only about where speech came from, but they also disagree about the exact reasons why so many languages exist. Edward Sapir, an American linguistic anthropologist, and Benjamin Lee Whorf, a decade later, focused on the various means of expression found in various cultures. They made some very important observations about spoken (and probably written) language, drawing their evidence primarily from the languages of primitive societies. First, the things that are most important to the values of each culture are reflected in subtle ways in human language. As a result, one could say that language is a reflection of culture, or, to put it another way, people seem to find ways to say what they need to say. The numerous words—or variations of words—that the Eskimos use to describe the various states of whale blubber provide a familiar illustration of on the whale, prepared for consumption—raw, cooked, rancid. The observation that drunk has more synonyms than any other English word is another example. This seems to be the result of a psychological need to euphemize something that is unpleasant, uncomfortable, or taboo. This is a technique that is also used to describe other words that seem important but are wrong behavior or aspects of culture.

Language adaptability Another observation is that almost anything that can be said in any other language can be said in any known language without much change. This may require a lot of circumlocution and some nonverbal vocalization, but even if the idea is foreign to the original language, it can be expressed clearly in another culture's language. Similar to how anthropologists have been able to explain specifics of Western technology to people in distant cultures, students of linguistic anthropology have been able to adequately describe the esoteric linguistic propositions of primitive societies in English. Since spoken language is seen as a cultural artifact, it can be seen as a universal means of communication that different societies use in different ways to speed up and define the many points of contact between people.

However, language is still a phenomenon that is only partially understood and is used in a variety of discourses. There are a number of criteria that have been used to categorize language. On the basis of their informative, dynamic, emotional, and aesthetic functions, one scheme established four categories. The narrative aspects of meaning are the primary focus of informative communication; The exchange of dispositions like opinions and attitudes in dynamic discourse The emotive use of language involves evoking other people's feelings in order to motivate them to act; and stylistic aspects of expression are conveyed through aesthetic discourse, which is typically regarded as a poetic quality in speech.

The phenomenon of laughter as a form of communication is in a category of its own, with its closest relative being its apparent opposite, crying, despite the fact that the majority of vocal sounds other than words are typically considered prelinguistic language. In instances where aggression is thwarted and laugh-like phenomena appear to result among herds, twentieth-century ethnologists, such as Konrad Lorenz, attempted to link laughter with group behavior among animals. Although they appear reasonable, Lorenz's metaphors cannot be inductively verified. Many people find them to be less plausible than the more common theories of Sigmund Freud, an Austrian neurologist, and others that laughter is caused by the unconscious release of tensions or inhibitions. Laughter is a highly effective, useful, and contagious means of vocal communication that is developed in the infant as a form of self-generated pleasure and rewarded both physically and psychologically by feelings of satisfaction. Similar to how crying, an infantile and probably instinctive response to discomfort, conveys an unmistakable emotional state to others, it addresses a wide range of cultural issues, frequently more effectively than speech.

Philosophers and psychologists respond in different ways to the question of why people laugh in difficult social situations. Based on his research into court comedies written in France in the 18th century, the English novelist George Meredith proposed the idea that laughing is an enjoyable form of social correction. The philosopher Henri Bergson's hypothesis that laughter is a form of rebellion against the mechanization of human behavior and nature and Freud's concept of laughter as repressed sexual feeling are the two most well-known modern theories of the social sources of laughter. Arthur Koestler, a writer, believed that laughing could lead to personal enlightenment, revelation, and then freedom from ambiguity or misinterpretation regarding a particular aspect of the environment.

As a means of communication, the human vocal instrument represents a turning point in both physical and intellectual development. It is capable of expressing the most fundamental instinctual needs as well as a variety of highly intellectual processes, including the potential mastery of numerous languages with extensive vocabularys. Talented individuals are able to perform tricks like ventriloquism and mimicry of other voices, as well as mimic the sounds of nature through song thanks to the vocal mechanism's ability to imitate (including its cortical directors). The ability of singers to accompany their own voices in different keys to produce effects of electronic duets or choruses composed from one person's voice has been extended even further by recent tape recording techniques.

Prerequisites for mass communication The technology of modern mass communication is the result of the convergence of a variety of discoveries and inventions, some of which, like the printing press, actually came before the Industrial Revolution. The newer forms of mass communication, particularly broadcasting, were developed through technological ingenuity in the 19th and 20th centuries. Without this innovation, the near-global distribution of printed words, images, and sounds would not be possible today. Before public communication in its current form could occur, the steam printing press, radio, motion pictures, television, sound recording, and systems of mass production and distribution were required.

However, mass communication's development in the West did not rely solely on technology. Before massive publishing and newspaper empires could use existing communications technology to meet widespread demands for popular reading materials, a large population of literate citizens was required. The radio, television, film, and recording industries—the institutions that are most highly developed in wealthy, industrial nations—were and remain dependent on wealth and interest. Before this persuasion is accepted by the general public, certain minimal economic and educational standards must be met even in nations where public communication is primarily used for government propaganda.

Control of mass communication Over time, a relatively small number of professional communicators, who appear to be able to reach an ever-increasing number of people as populations grow and interest grows, have taken control of the tools of mass communication. Some argue that this number is shrinking. For instance, there are fewer newspapers serving more readers than ever before in the United States, and a small number of book publishers produce the majority of bestsellers.

However, when it comes to serving the general public, public communicators do not always have complete discretion. The nature and quantity of the products and services that are produced and distributed are constrained, just like in any other market, by consumer satisfaction—or lack thereof. Laws governing libel, slander, and invasion of privacy place restrictions on mass communicators. Additionally, most nations have professional traditions that entail responsibilities for those who maintain public access. Government regulations limit privileges to use broadcasting frequencies in either a loose or rigid manner in almost every modern nation. Print and film media operate under strict government control in certain regions, and national agencies in some nations have complete control over all broadcasting. Written and film communications may be subject to censorship restrictions imposed by local law and similar to those imposed on other private businesses. Publishers and filmmakers, on the other hand, are subject to varying degrees of decorum and self-censorship, typically based on the target audiences for their content.

Public opinion on political issues, as well as personal lifestyles and preferences, consumer behavior, children's sensibilities and dispositions, and potential incitements to violence, are all topics of heated debate regarding the impact of public communication on audiences. There is a wide range of opinion regarding these matters. Some people believe that the effects of mass communication as a whole are generally harmless to people of all ages. The theory that mass communication only seems to change attitudes and behavior when it reinforces the status quo— that is, It has an effect on values that are already prevalent and accepted in the culture. Other researchers, most of whom focus on psychological or psychiatric fields, are of the opinion that mass communications are powerful tools for informal education and persuasion. The majority of their findings stem from their observations that, in technological societies, messages sent to them through public communication influence people's personal views of social realities beyond their immediate experience.

It ignores a lot of common experience to assume that public communication primarily reflects current values, morals, and attitudes. This view cannot be supported by the obvious and direct influence of media, film, and television content on fashion, fads, and small talk. As a tool for commercial advertising, public communication has also consistently and clearly performed well. There is evidence to suggest that different methods of mass communication have different effects on different parts of the audience. These effects appear to be too numerous and short-lived for current instruments to accurately measure. Although many psychologists believe that the nature of children's play experiences is crucial to their maturation, the majority of the vast output on television, radio, and print probably only serves as "play" and has little impact on adult behavior.

When it comes to the voting habits of the so-called "undecided voters," it is fairly well established that television, newspapers, and periodicals influence political opinion. Numerous studies have demonstrated that middle-of-the-road voters frequently hold the balance of power that determines the outcomes of elections, despite the fact that the majority of citizens in the United States cast their votes in accordance with social, educational, and economic determinants as well as party lines. Politicians have developed an awareness of the images they see on television and have developed a significant portion of their campaign strategy with the television audience in mind. Campaign planning and brand development have been brought into the political arena by television-savvy advertising agencies. Television campaigns' efficacy cannot yet be reliably assessed.

Modernity necessitates almost ubiquitous public communication. Most dependable overviews show that most individuals of the world (counting those of authoritarian nations) are normally happy with the sort of mass correspondence accessible to them. The majority of people appear to accept what they are presented with no qualms because there are no alternatives to the communication that they readily and conveniently receive. For the majority of people, mass communication is just one aspect of life, as home and daily work are their primary concerns. Public communication is a low-cost addition to daily life that typically targets low common denominators of taste, interest, and perception refinement. The traditional requirements for popular approval and assent have generally prevented the use of mass communication for overt subversion of culturally sanctioned institutions, despite the fact that it places a significant amount of power in the hands of a relatively small number of individuals. Critics occasionally express a fear of such subversion.

The psychology of communication Since World War II, contemporary psychologists have shown a lot of interest in the ways that people communicate. Behaviorists have a propensity to interpret communication in terms of stimulus-response relationships between the people or groups that receive it and the people or groups that send it. Communicational interactions are typically viewed by those who adhere to Freud's analysis of group psychology and ego theory as reverberations of early family group dynamics.

By the middle of the 1950s, the main focus of psychological research had shifted to the persuasive qualities of various types of messages. Psychologists have tried to find out if "persuasibility," a general trait of personality, can be found in people as a whole. However, with some caveats, it would appear that people are indeed variable persuaders and that this quality is sometimes linked to personality traits.

In an effort to explain not only the ways in which communication changed attitudes but also the reasons for resistance to change, other psychologists have investigated the recipients of communication and the advancing concepts of "selective perception," "selective attention," and "selective retention." The dynamics of rumor communication, the effects of "scare messages," the degree of credulity provided by sources of prestige value, and the influence of group consensus on individual perceptions of communications were among their areas of interest.

A theory of what is known as "cognitive dissonance," which is based on the observation that most people cannot tolerate more than a specific degree of inconsistency in the environments they perceive, may encompass some of the suggestions that emerged from the work of certain modern psychologists. A person who thinks he or she is a great bowler but once gets a very low score is one example of cognitive dissonance. The bowler's knowledge of his skill and the fact that he scored a low score are examples of the dissonant or inconsistent elements. Tension results from this. The bowler may alter his behavior or misinterpret or reinterpret the dissonant elements to lessen the difference between the facts in order to reduce this tension—dissonance. He might, for instance, attribute his performance to the bowling alley, the bowling ball, or the room's temperature. As a result, he tries to find mental equilibrium.

The communication psychologist finds this shift in perception of reality to be of fundamental interest. The major criterion for the psychological analysis of communication is not the message or the medium, but rather the expectation of the person receiving the message. This is because the agreement or disagreement of a communication with an individual's cognitive structure affects not only behavior but also perception.

There is no reason to believe that any of the theories of audience psychology that have been presented thus far—such as those of Gestaltists, Freudians, behaviorists, and others—are irrelevant to comprehending the processes of communication. However, none appears to fully account for all of the effects of communications on individuals. The numerous aspects of communication pose significant challenges for upcoming psychological research and theory.

In phonetics, glottal stop is a brief check on the airstream caused by stopping the vibration of the vocal cords by closing the glottis (the space between the vocal cords). Upon release, an explosive sound resembling a choke or cough is heard. Although it is one of the allophones of the t phoneme in some dialects (such as the Cockney or Brooklynese "bo'l" for "bottle"), the glottal stop is not a distinct sound in English. However, many other languages, including Arabic and many American Indian languages, use it as a phoneme. Glottalization refers to the temporary partial or complete closure of the glottis. The closure may take place simultaneously with the primary articulation, slightly after it, or a little bit before it. Glottalized stops and sibilants are found in a number of African and American Indian languages, as are glottalized vowels.

Aeolic dialect, any of the various ancient Greek dialects spoken in Thessaly, Boeotia, and Asiatic Aeolis after about 1000 BCE, including the island of Lesbos, where mainland Aeolian colonists established their cities. The neighboring West Greek (Doric) dialects influenced the West Thessalian and Boeotian varieties of Aeolic, while Ionic influenced Asiatic Aeolic. Alcaeus, a lesbian poet (circa 620–c. 580 BCE), as well as Sappho c. 610–c. 580 BCE) spoke an Asiatic Aeolic dialect, whereas Corinna, a Boeotian poet (fl. c. 500 BCE?) used her native Boeotian language.

Foundations of Relationships By distinguishing between our social and personal relationships, we can begin to classify important relationships (VanLear, Koerner, & Allen, 2006). Because they are intimate, close, and interdependent relationships like those we have with best friends, partners, or our immediate family, personal relationships satisfy our emotional, relational, and instrumental needs. Social relationships lack the closeness and interdependence of personal relationships and only occasionally meet our needs. Coworkers, distant relatives, and friends are all examples of social relationships. The question of whether or not relationships are voluntary is another distinction that can be used to classify them. For instance, some personal relationships, like those with romantic partners, are voluntary, while others, like those with close siblings, are involuntary.

Stages of Relational Interaction Communication is at the heart of how we form relationships with other people. The everyday conversations and other seemingly insignificant interactions that make up the foundation of our relationships are how we achieve the achievement of relating. Given that partners in relationships do not enter each encounter or relationship with expectations that are compatible with one another, it is through our communication that we adapt to the dynamic nature of our relational worlds. We are able to test and be tested by both potential and existing relationships through communication. We also respond when someone violates or fails to meet those expectations through communication (Knapp & Vangelisti, 2009).

Initiating During the initiating stage, individuals evaluate one another and make an effort to appear favorable. Whether you meet someone in the school hallway or in the produce section of the grocery store, you scan them and think about your expectations for the situation, any prior knowledge you may have of them, and so on. Several factors influence initiating.

You can introduce yourself by saying, "Hi, my name is Rich." You may simply ask, "What's up?" if you meet someone you already know. You have already been through this before. Initiation is also affected by time constraints. A casual passing requires a brief greeting, whereas a scheduled meeting may necessitate a more formal start. The length of time since your last encounter will affect your initiation if you already know the person. For instance, if you see a high school friend while they are home for the winter break, you might set aside a significant amount of time to catch up; But if you see someone at work with whom you just spoke ten minutes before, you might not bother to talk to them. We communicate differently in a crowded bar than we do on an airplane, which has an impact on how we start conversations. Even with all of this variation, people at this stage typically follow typical social interaction scripts.

Experimenting (Knapp & Vangelisti, 2009) The researchers who developed these relational stages compared the experimenting stage, in which individuals exchange information and frequently move from being strangers to acquaintances, to the "sniffing ritual" of animals. As the experimenting phase begins, it is typical to have a basic exchange of information. On the first day of class, for instance, you might have a conversation with the person sitting next to you and take turns telling them about your major, hometown, residence hall, and year in school. After that, you can try new things and see if there are any interests you share. Once you find out that you both like the St. Louis Cardinals, you might talk more about baseball and other things you like to do; However, the experiment may occasionally fail. During the experimenting stage, if you attempt to exchange information with another person and are met with silence or hesitation, you may interpret this as an indication that you shouldn't pursue further interactions with them.

In existing relationships, experiments continue. Young adults who catch up with their parents when they return home for a visit or committed couples who recount their day while preparing dinner frequently engage in the type of small talk that is characteristic of the experimenting stage. When you feel like you have to make small talk to be polite, it can be annoying at times. Even when I am wearing earbuds, I have discovered that strangers sometimes feel the need to talk to me at the gym. I engage in small talk in accordance with social norms of cheerfulness and politeness, despite my desire to skip the small talk and just work out. Small talk is useful for a number of important purposes, including establishing a conversational starting point that can lead people to uncover topics of conversation that go beyond the surface level, assisting us in auditioning someone to determine whether we would like to talk to them further, and generally fostering a sense of ease and community with other people. According to the authors of this model of relationships (Knapp & Vangelisti, 2009), the majority of our relationships do not progress much beyond this point, even though small talk is not considered to be very substantive.

Intensifying When we enter the intensifying stage, we indicate that we would like or are open to more intimacy. Before we attempt more intimacy, we wait for a sign of acceptance. This gradual increase in intimacy can last for weeks, months, or years and may involve inviting a new friend to a party, dinner at your place, or a vacation with you. Even if the experimentation stage went well, inviting a person you are still getting to know on vacation without first having a less intimate conversation would be seen as odd. In this stage, steady progress is essential to save face and avoid overly exposing ourselves. Requesting and granting favors can also contribute to the intensification of a relationship, along with spending more time together on a personal level. A good example of this is when one friend helps another get ready for a big birthday party. However, the relationship may become unbalanced if one party asks for too many favors or does not return favors. This could lead to a transition to a different stage, such as differentiating.

The development of nicknames, personal idioms, and inside jokes are additional indicators of the stage's intensifying nature; more use of "we" and "our"; increased disclosure of one another's identities, such as when someone says, "My friends all think you are really laid back and easy to get along with" and a loosening of typical restrictions on personal space and possessions (for instance, you can go to the apartment of your best friend if your roommate is getting on your nerves). As new expectations for relationships emerge, it can be challenging to navigate the shifting boundaries between individuals at this stage, which can result in conflict or uncertainty regarding the relationship's future. Relational integration may result from successfully managing this growing closeness.

During the integrating stage, the identities and personalities of two people combine, and a sense of dependence emerges. This stage is most evident in romantic relationships, but there are aspects that are present in other types of relationships as well. The merging of two people's social networks is one of the verbal and nonverbal indicators of the integrating stage; People who aren't in the relationship start treating the people in the relationship as if they were one person (for example, always saying, "Let's invite Olaf and Bettina"); or the partners in a relationship present themselves as a single entity (for instance, by opening a joint bank account or signing a single holiday card). Spending time with friends and family on their own helps two people balance their needs for connection and independence even as they become more integrated.

During the bonding stage, there is a public ceremony that makes the official commitment known. Weddings, commitment ceremonies, and civil unions are examples of such rituals. Clearly, this stage only applies to romantic couples almost exclusively. The bonding ritual can take place at any point in a relationship, making it arbitrary in some ways. In point of fact, when a relationship fails, bonding rituals are frequently canceled or reversed, possibly due to insufficient time spent on the experimenting or integrating phases. However, the symbolic act of bonding can have very real effects on how two people communicate about and perceive their relationship, so it deserves its own stage. For instance, if conflict or stress threatens the relationship, the couple and those in their social network may be motivated to maintain it with greater diligence due to the formality of the bond.

At any point in the relational interaction model, distinguishing between individual differences can be difficult; However, during the differentiation stage, the primary focus shifts to communicating these differences. As we and our return to I and my, differentiation is the opposite of integration. Prior to the integration of the current relationship, individuals may attempt to rebound from previous relationships or possessions. For instance, Carrie might say, "I'm having my friends over to the apartment and would like to have privacy for the evening," to reclaim friends who became "shared" as she got closer to Julie, her roommate, and their social networks merged. A relationship that began before the individuals knew each other sufficiently well may begin to differentiate. Unpleasant discoveries about the other person's past, personality, or values during the integrating or experimenting stage could lead a person to begin differentiating, even in relationships where the bonding stage is less likely to occur, such as friendships.

The Oxford English Dictionary Online defines circumscribing as "drawing a line around something or putting a boundary around it." As a result, during the circumscribing stage, individuals verbally isolate themselves from one another, which results in a decrease in communication and a restriction on particular topics or areas. They might say, "I don't want to talk about that anymore" or "You mind your business, I'll mind mine." Verbal expressions of commitment may go unheard—for instance, when one person says, "I know we've had some problems lately, but I still like being with you," and the other person responds with silence—if one person was more interested in differentiating in the previous stage or if the desire to end the relationship is unilateral.

Stagnant During the stagnant phase, the relationship may come to a halt as both parties essentially wait for the relationship to end. Internal communication may occur frequently while external communication may be avoided. Mindreading's relational conflict flaw occurs when a person's internal thoughts cause them to avoid communicating. A person might, for instance, consider the following: "There is no need to bring this up again, because I know exactly how he will react!" In some relationships, this stage can last for a long time. Friends who want to end a relationship but are unsure how to do so, couples who are separated and waiting for a divorce, and parents and children who are estranged may experience prolonged periods of stagnation. In the experimental stage, after a failed exchange, there may be brief periods of stagnation in which you may be in a difficult situation but the other person is still there. Even though the majority of people don't like to stay in this uncomfortable stage, some may do so to avoid the potential pain of ending the relationship, others may still hope to rekindle the spark that started the relationship, and still others may enjoy leading their relationship partner on.

Avoiding When people indicate that they want to cut off communication, moving into the avoiding stage may be a way to end the awkwardness that comes with stagnation. In the avoiding stage, communication can be very direct, such as "I don't want to talk to you anymore," or it can be more indirect, such as "I have to meet someone in a short while, so I can't talk long." Physical avoidance, such as leaving a room or asking for a change in the work schedule, may help us clearly communicate our desire to end the relationship, but that is not always an option. People may engage in cognitive dissociation, which means they mentally shut down and ignore the other person even though they are still physically copresent, in situations such as a parent-child relationship, where the child is still dependent on the parent, or a roommate relationship, where a lease agreement prevents the roommate from leaving.

The terminating stage of a relationship can occur shortly after its initiation or after a relationship has existed for ten to twenty years. External factors like geographical separation or internal factors like shifting values or personalities that weaken the bond can lead to termination. Termination exchanges typically begin with a summary message that summarizes the relationship and explains why it is ending (for example, "We've had some ups and downs over our three years together, but I'm getting ready to go to college, and I either want to be with someone who is willing to support me, or I want to be free to explore who I am."). Termination exchanges involve some typical elements of communication. The summary message might be followed by a distance message that elaborates on the drift in the relationship (for instance, "We've really grown apart over the past year"), which might then be followed by a disassociation message that helps people get ready for being apart by projecting what will happen when the relationship ends (for example, "I know you'll do fine without me"). You can take advantage of this opportunity to investigate your options and decide whether or not to enroll in college. Last but not least, there is frequently a message about the possibility of further communication in the relationship (for instance, "I think it would be best if we don't see each other for the first few months, but text me if you want to.") 2009, Knapp and Vangelisti). Understanding the intricate processes that influence relational formation and deterioration is made possible by these ten stages of relational development. We also weigh the costs and benefits when making decisions about our relationships.

According to Harvey & Wenzel (2006), social exchange theory basically entails weighing the costs and benefits of a given relationship. The outcomes of a relationship that benefit us in some way are referred to as rewards, while the costs range from offering favors to providing emotional support. When we do not receive the outcomes or rewards that we believe we deserve, we may have a negative perception of the relationship or, at the very least, a particular exchange or moment in the relationship, and believe that we are not benefiting enough. Costs and benefits are balanced in an equitable relationship, which typically results in a positive relationship evaluation and satisfaction.

According to social exchange theory, commitment and interdependence are crucial interpersonal and psychological aspects of a relationship. The relationship between a person's well-being and involvement in a particular relationship is referred to as interdependence. In a relationship, interdependence is felt when: (1) satisfaction is high or important needs are met; (2) There are no viable alternatives, implying that the individual's requirements would not be met without the relationship; or, if there is a high level of investment in the relationship, resources may decrease or disappear without it (Harvey & Wenzel, 2006).

However, we should not view social exchange theory as an accounting of costs and benefits in a tit-for-tat fashion (Noller, 2006). If we carried around a small notepad and wrote down each favor or good deed we performed so that we could anticipate its repayment, we wouldn't be very good relationship partners. We are all aware, as was mentioned earlier, at some point in our relationships, but that awareness is not persistent. We also have communal relationships, in which members work together for the benefit of each other and do good deeds or favors for nothing in return (Harvey & Wenzel, 2006). By simply enjoying the relationship, we may engage communally without even realizing it as the dynamics of the relationship change. When a relationship is in conflict, it has been suggested that we become more aware of the costs and benefits balance (Noller, 2006). In general, there is a greater likelihood that a relationship will succeed if there is contentment and commitment, which means that we are pleased in a relationship either intrinsically or by the rewards we receive.

The Importance of Effective Interpersonal Communication in the Workplace On a scale from one to five, managers place the importance of having effective interpersonal communication skills at 4.37, just below the "ability to work in teams" mark.

They are highly prized for a variety of reasons; Even though the majority of business in the workplace is now conducted online, verbal communication skills are still required to work well with coworkers and managers.

As a result, interpersonal skills are absolutely necessary for business success. Let's now examine why effective interpersonal communication is essential to your professional advancement and workplace productivity.

1. Problem-solving skills are important because they allow people to talk about problems and weigh the benefits and drawbacks of different options before choosing the best one.

For instance, brainstorming exercises are examples of situations where interpersonal communication is necessary because it is critical that everyone feels respected and is allowed to express their thoughts, ideas, and opinions.

2. Alignment with business objectives Poor employee-employer communication can have a number of negative effects on the company. Workers may quickly become disengaged from the company's objectives and become frustrated if leaders and managers fail to clearly communicate tasks.

In addition, many workers claim that their supervisors fail to provide them with clear objectives and directions for their work.

As a result, managers ought to be able to continuously align employees with the business strategy through effective online and offline communication as well as the appropriate tools for internal communication.

3. Trust According to the American Psychological Association, only about half of employees in the United States believe that their managers are honest with them.

Some of the most common reasons for poor workplace communication are a lack of trust and transparency.

All employees, particularly business leaders, should improve their communication with their employees because interpersonal communication skills are essential for enhancing workplace communication and trust.

4. Change management During efforts to manage change within an organization, effective interpersonal communication is crucial.

Employees benefit from better understanding, alignment, and collaborative work toward the successful implementation of the change as a result of effective employee communication.

5. Culture of the company Good interpersonal relationships are crucial to the success of an organization's culture.

The culture of an organization becomes more positive and synergistic when employees have strong interpersonal communication skills. Negativity, confusion, and disagreements, on the other hand, are unavoidable when interpersonal relationships are poor.

In the end, this wrecks the workplace, lowers employee output, and hurts the bottom line of the business.

6. Employee recognition is fueled by effective interpersonal communication. Employees are more likely to recognize one another's good work and provide constructive feedback when they have good interpersonal relationships with their managers.

7. Misunderstandings in the workplace Managers who maintain professionalism, open communication in the workplace, and a positive

attitude are more likely to be viewed as approachable by their staff.

Misunderstandings, gossip, and rumors in the workplace are much less likely to occur when employees have the confidence to speak candidly with decision-makers.

8. Relationships with others In the workplace, building and maintaining meaningful relationships with others requires excellent interpersonal skills.

As a result, people who have strong interpersonal communication skills are better able to work in teams and establish positive relationships with their coworkers.

9. Management and leadership that work well An effective leader needs to be able to build trust, build interpersonal relationships, and communicate clearly.

Employees will likely be irritated and confused by a manager who lacks interpersonal communication skills. In point of fact, managers need to work on their interpersonal skills more than the average employee.

10. To ensure the success of their employees, managers must also possess strong interpersonal communication skills. Leaders need to be able to teach their employees the right skills so that they can accomplish their responsibilities and the company's objectives.

Additionally, they ought to be the ones imparting interpersonal communication skills to their employees.

11. Management of conflict Conflicts are commonplace in the workplace, and we cannot always expect our employees to resolve them calmly and promptly. Interpersonal communication becomes increasingly important for resolving such conflicts.

Communication between people is essential to conflict management. In point of fact, all conflict management techniques that make use of communication to calm situations in stressful settings are significantly more effective.

12. Career advancement Since many employers are looking for workers with good communication skills, many employees can advance their careers by constantly improving their interpersonal communication skills.

In addition, a Workforce Solutions Group survey revealed that over 60% of employers believe applicants lack sufficient interpersonal and communication skills to be considered for jobs.

Employees and communicators now have to adapt to the new trends in employee communication due to the increasing prevalence of communication technologies.

13. Remote work This year, we have all witnessed the significance of workplace communication.

Interpersonal communication among peers, coworkers, managers, and leaders has been disrupted by the rise of remote work. However, its significance has never been greater.

Even when employees are physically dispersed, employers must continue to encourage engaging workplace conversations in order to maintain open and transparent cultures.

14. Crisis management Many employers will remember 2020 as the year of crisis management in addition to remote work. The capacity to foster interpersonal communication within the workplace is one of the characteristics of businesses that manage crises more effectively.

It is much simpler for businesses to convey the impact of the crisis on a personal and organizational level when employees are connected and able to work together effectively.

Interpersonal Communication and Remote Work
The fact that many organizations are adopting remote work practices has also sparked numerous inquiries regarding how to adapt workplace communications to this new circumstance.

We are all aware that remote work is completely reshaping the way our employees communicate, despite the fact that interpersonal communication is frequently equated with in-person communication.

Employers are now looking for new ways to keep their workforce connected, engaged, and well-informed in order to adapt to this new trend. In addition, employers need to be aware that there is no one-size-fits-all approach to internal communications because many workers are currently experiencing a significant amount of information overload.

They need to know how to use the channels for internal communications and how to make communication more personalized based on the locations, languages, titles, and responsibilities of employees, as well as their interests.

As a result, many are putting new, cutting-edge employee communication solutions into use. These solutions provide a centralized location for keeping remote, white-collar, and in-office employees connected, as well as for daily, meaningful, two-way company conversations.

Six Key Components of Interpersonal Communication According to communication theory, interpersonal communication consists of six key components.

Both the sender and the receiver of the information are referred to as communicators. At least two people are involved in a conversation in interpersonal communication.

The message The message is one of the most crucial aspects of interpersonal communication. There are numerous ways to convey a message: speech, body language, tone of voice, gestures, and other indicators are all examples of noise.

Noise is the gap between what is sent and what is received. Jargon, language barriers, inattention, and a variety of other things are examples of noise. Many businesses face noise issues in the workplace, which is why internal communicators have trouble getting the necessary employees' attention.

The response of the receiver is called feedback. To put it another way, it's the message that is returned to the sender. Feedback is crucial because it enables the sender to determine whether the message was received and correctly interpreted.

Context A message's correct reception and interpretation are largely determined by context. Interpersonal communication is therefore contextual. The environmental factors that influence the outcomes of communication are the subject of context.

Time and location are two examples, as are gender, culture, personal interests, and the environment. Finally, this interpersonal communication aspect refers to how communication takes place. A particular channel, or medium, is used to send and receive messages.

Emails and intranets are two of the most widely used forms of workplace communication in addition to face-to-face interactions. Employers must pay close attention to the effectiveness of these channels of communication in order to make informed decisions.

According to research that was published in the journal Business Communication Quarterly, "10 Must-Have Interpersonal Communication Skills," "soft skills" are interpersonal qualities like "people skills," while "hard skills" are the technical expertise that is required for a job.

With 77% of employers stating that soft skills are just as important as hard skills, employers all over the world are becoming more aware of the significance of soft skills.

Despite the fact that they are frequently more challenging to identify and quantify, these are just as crucial to career advancement, team and individual morale, and business success.

The aforementioned study outlines ten essential soft skills that business executives regard as essential. These are some:

Communication – oral, written, presenting, listening Courtesy – business etiquette, manners, saying please and thank you, being respectful Flexibility – adaptability, willingness to change, lifelong learner, accepting new things, adapting, teachable Integrity – honest, ethical, high morals, has personal values Interpersonal skills – nice, personable, sense of humour, friendly, empathetic, positive Attitude – optimistic, enthusiastic, encouraging, happy, confident Professional

People feel disconnected and excluded in the workplace when interpersonal communication is poor, and they are unable to freely voice their desires, needs, and concerns.

This can be a big issue, especially for remote and dispersed, non-wired employees in global organizations. Employees should always be able to communicate with their coworkers in a matter of seconds, even when they are unable to meet in person.

On the other hand, employers and internal communicators ought to be able to send messages to the entire organization that are personalized, timely, and pertinent, as well as increase engagement with internal content.

Skillset Map of a Modern Internal Communication Department In this blog, we have talked about how important it is to learn how to communicate with others in a professional setting.

However, in order to engage, connect, and keep employees informed, successful communicators, including leaders and internal communications departments, require additional skills and knowledge.

One of the most important strategic business partners today are professionals in internal communications, and their role in keeping workplaces engaged, safe, informed, and productive has increased over the past few years.

More specifically, communication professionals need new knowledge in the following areas in addition to having excellent interpersonal communication skills:

With Haiilo, Business Technology Communication People, Research, and Analytics can make internal communications more strategic. In today's world, where workplace trends are constantly changing, internal communications should be considered one of the most important strategic partners.

Organizations must adapt their internal communication strategy to new trends and employee preferences in order to keep their employees informed, motivated, connected, and productive.

Leaders, managers, and internal communications professionals can use the Haiilo employee communication solution to:

Create personalized news feeds for employees based on their roles, interests, locations, and preferences. Keep remote and deskless employees connected to the rest of the workplace. Provide easy mobile access to all important company information. Encourage employee-generated content. Encourage external content sharing and brand ambassadorship. Connect various internal communication channels such as email, intranet, document sharing, and private messaging solutions.

Criticism In 1992, a chapter in Communication Yearbook No. 15 argued that the concept of "intrapersonal communication" is flawed. [citation needed] The chapter first listed the various definitions. It would appear that a series of logical and linguistic flaws lead to intrapersonal communication. The term "intrapersonal communication" itself is ambiguous: Since many definitions borrow, apply, and thereby distort conceptual features (such as sender, receiver, message, and dialogue) from typical interpersonal communication, they appear to be circular. The so-called "intrapersonal" exchange is allegedly carried out by unknown parties or entities; There are a lot of instances in which a very private language is proposed that, upon investigation, turns out to be completely inaccessible and ultimately unjustifiable. In general, the tendency to interpret the inner mental processes that come before and accompany our communicative behaviors as if they were yet another type of communication seems to be the source of intrapersonal communication. The overall point is that this reconstruction of our inner mental processes in everyday public conversational language and idioms is highly dubious and, at best, tenuous.

Ludwig Wittgenstein (1889–1951) used a thought experiment to introduce a set of arguments against a hypothetical uniquely constructed "private language," such as intended to be understood only by the author, in his later works, particularly the Philosophical Investigations. According to the arguments, such language would be essentially incoherent (even for the author). Even if the author initially believed to fully comprehend the intended meaning of their writings at the time of writing, subsequent readings may be fraught with misremembering the meaning intended by one's previous self, resulting in misreading, misinterpretation, and misdirectedness. For the continuous maintenance of the flux of linguistic meaning, the only convention that provides a relatively stabilizing factor is consensus-based convention. According to this point of view, language can only be seen as a social activity by definition.

Interior monologue is a similar term in literature and literary criticism. Occasionally, this is used interchangeably with stream of consciousness: [51] The Oxford Dictionary of Literary Terms states that "they can also be distinguished psychologically and literarily." [Citation needed] a narrative mode or method that attempts to depict the numerous thoughts and feelings that pass through the mind. "while an interior monologue always presents a character's thoughts 'directly,' without the apparent intervention of a summarizing and selecting narrator, it does not necessarily mingle them with impressions and perceptions, nor does it necessarily violate the norms of grammar, or logic – but the stream of consciousness technique also does one or both of these things." [Citation needed] In a psychological sense, "stream of consciousness is the subject matter, while interior monologue is the technique for

The Seven Essential Elements of the Communication Process Having strong communication skills is essential for success in nearly any field. Professionals who succeed understand the significance of communication. They know the procedure and how, if used correctly, it will help them succeed at work and in life.

The seven essential components of effective communication are listed below.

1. Sender The individual attempting to convey a message is the sender.

The sender wants the recipient to comprehend and receive their message. The message usually aims to get the other person or people involved to do or understand something.

Unfortunately, when information is transferred, the recipient may not comprehend the intended meaning of the message. In point of fact, it is not uncommon for the other person or people to respond affirmatively, indicating that the message was received. This does not imply that the sender intended for the message to be understood.

2. The recipient is the person who receives the message. As the recipient, they are responsible for converting the words into thoughts, analyzing

those thoughts, and deciding how to respond to the sender.

The problem is that words frequently have different meanings depending on the recipient's education and experience.

3. Message Regardless of how carefully you choose to speak, the other person will only hear a small amount of what you have to say. In fact, the literature asserts that words convey the least value.

As a result, body language and voice inflection are more effective communicators than words. Communication is occurring even when no words are spoken. A message is being sent when someone frowns, avoids eye contact, or looks at their watch—and it might not be the intended message.

Therefore, it makes sense to pay attention to voice inflection and body language. This requires more than merely listening and watching. To be most effective, we need to give it our full attention.

Congruency, or agreement, between the words, meaning, and emotion is what makes a message effective. Congruency can only be achieved through effective body language and voice inflection.

4. The medium through which the sender transmits the message to the recipient is the channel. This could be done in person, over the phone, by email, text message, written communication, or through a third party.

It is essential to keep in mind that the most crucial aspect of communication—body language—is missed when communication is solely verbal.

Body language and voice inflection are not included if the communication is written.

Therefore, a sender will want to think about which medium to use based on the nature of the message. Meetings may be required for more pressing messages, while written or verbal communication may be sufficient for less pressing messages.

5. Interference that occurs during the communication process is referred to as noise. Noise may cause distractions for both the sender and the receiver. Internal noise (such as feelings, thoughts, and so on) may exist. or from outside sources (such as radio or other conversations).

Take steps to make noise less distracting when you hear it. Refocus for some time if the noise is internal. It may be helpful to take several deep breaths. It's possible that the mental break you need to clear your mind is to excuse yourself and go get some water.

If the noise comes from outside, try to move the meeting to a quieter location. Consider moving the meeting to a time when there are fewer distractions if necessary.

6. The process of determining whether the message was properly received is called feedback. The sender or the receiver can start this. For instance, the sender might request that the recipient repeat the message to ensure that it was received as intended. A good listener, on the other hand, will give feedback to make sure they understood what was being said.

There are four ways feedback can occur.

Paraphrasing comes first and is probably the most prevalent. Reciting what another person said in your own words is called paraphrasing.

The second one is a summary. This entails making a brief statement of the most important points and feelings that the other person has expressed.

The third is to express one's emotions. Emotions behind the message are more important than the message itself. Often, this is a good way to show empathy.

Reflecting meaning is the fourth approach. This kind of feedback aims to figure out what the other person is trying to say. Sometimes, a person will say one thing and mean another thing.

Made in the USA
Las Vegas, NV
28 September 2023